From Fatherless to Fearless II

Courageous Women Find Success When Married to a New Way

CANDICE CREAR

FOREWORD BY DR. KAREN TOWNSEND

From Fatherless to *Fearless* II

Courageous Women Find Success When Married to a New Way

CANDICE CREAR

FOREWORD BY DR. KAREN TOWNSEND

COPYRIGHT

Charismatic Publishing, Cincinnati, OH

Copyright © 2021 by Candice Crear

All rights reserved for collection of works. All authors reserve the right to their story. No part of this book may be reproduced or transmitted in any form or by any means without written permission of the author. Reviewers may quote brief passages in reviews.

Neither the author nor the publisher assumes any responsibility for errors, omissions, or contrary interpretations of the subject matter herein. Any perceived slight of any individual or organizations is purely unintentional.

Brand and product names are trademarks or registered trademarks of their respective owners.

Scriptures quotations taken from The Holy Bible, English Standard Version. Copyright © 2001 by Crossway Bibles, a publishing ministry of Good News Publishers. Scriptures quotations taken from the New King James Version®. Copyright © 1982 by Thomas Nelson. Used by permission. Scriptures quotations taken from the Holy Bible, New Living Translation. Copyright © 1996, 2004, 2007, 2013 by Tyndale House Foundation. Used by permission of Tyndale House Publishers Inc., Carol Stream, Illinois 60188. Scripture quotations taken from the Amplified® Bible (AMP), Copyright © 2015 by The Lockman Foundation. Used by permission. www.Lockman.org. Scriptures quotations taken from the Holy Bible: New International Version®. Copyright © 1973, 1978, 1984 by International Bible Society. Used by permission of Zondervan Publishing House. All rights reserved. Scripture quotations taken from the New American Standard Bible® (NASB), Copyright © 1960, 1962, 1963, 1968, 1971, 1972, 1973, 1975, 1977, 1995 by The Lockman Foundation. Used by permission. www.Lockman.org

Editor: Greta Barnes, Candice Crear, Tenita Johnson

Cover Design: Angie A.

ISBN: 978-0-9989306-6-4

LCCN: 2017919777

Printed in the United States of America

💍 DEDICATION 💍

*To all the fatherless daughters,
who are breaking generational curses, this book is for you.*

Other Books by Candice Crear:

Invisible Dad

Invisible God, I'm Waiting

From Fatherless to Fearless

On Your Mark, Get Set, Reset!

TABLE OF CONTENTS

Acknowledgments i

Foreword iii

Chapter 1: Something Bruised, Something Blessed 1
    Nina Nicole

Chapter 2: To Have and To Hold Onto 23
    Allison Retzlaff

Chapter 3: First Comes Love, Then Comes Rejection 43
    Tenita C. Johnson

Chapter 4: Divorcing the Monster of Trauma 63
    Shameka Green

Chapter 5: Marital Miss 81
    Latisha Roodbeen

Chapter 6: Worthy to Wed 97
    Pearl Smith

ACKNOWLEDGMENTS

Giving all glory and honor to God, Whom provided the vision and provision to make this book come to fruition. To all of my anthology sisters who were vulnerable and bold enough to stand in their truth, I love and celebrate you.

💍 FOREWORD 💍

My mother was married.

And divorced.

Twice.

All before I turned nine years old.

As a result, I grew up as a *fatherless daughter.*

I didn't think it really impacted me. After all, you can't miss what you never had. Right?

Wrong.

Being "fatherless" not only impacted my "daughter" experience. It also impacted my "wife" experience.

You see, when your mother doesn't have a husband, and when you grow up without a father, you have no point of reference as it relates to what a husband is and what role he plays in the family. You don't have the benefit of mom *and* dad parenting together. So, when you grow up, get married and have children of your own, you lack the necessary "playbook" to effectively "partner and parent" with your spouse.

That was my situation. I am the mother of two daughters. I recall on more occasions than I would like to admit telling my husband how to "father" our daughters.

While he understood the important role that he played as a "Girl Dad," I was getting in the way of him doing it his way.

I told him how to talk to the girls.

I told him how to interact with the girls.

I told him that he should take the girls on "Daddy-Daughter Dates."

Then, one day, I realized that everything I was "telling" him to do represented everything I had longed for my absent father to do *for* and *with* me.

I wanted my husband to affirm my daughters because my father wasn't in my life to affirm *me*.

I wanted my husband to tell my daughters they were beautiful, precious and smart because, as a result of my father's absence, I didn't hear those things during my formative years.

I wanted my husband to be the first man my daughters fell in love with. I wanted him to set the standard. To be the example of what a "good man" does and is. I now recognize that, by not having that example, I often went "looking for love in all the wrong places!"

While few women want to talk about it, fatherless daughters need to discuss the impact of fatherlessness on their lives, their relationships and, yes, even their marriages. We are all products of our upbringing. For those of us who were brought up without our fathers, we bring that void into our marriages.

Candice Crear's latest project—*From Fatherless to Fearless: Married to a New Way*—is the book fatherless daughters have long needed—even if they didn't realize or recognize that they needed it.

While we may appear to have it all together, many of us are challenged daily because of an important piece that was missing from our lives. That piece being our fathers. And for far too many of us, without that *piece,* we haven't had *peace*...in our lives, in our relationships, and in our marriages. But now, Candice has given us the playbook we didn't know we needed!

Six courageous women have come together to share their stories.

Stories of sadness...and solace.

Stories of hurt...and healing.

Stories of longing, loss...and love.

And through these insightful and impactful stories, I believe you will be able to identify what pieces have been missing from your life, so you can have peace in all areas of your life.

Prepare to view yourself, your husband and marriage...*in a new way*!

Karen M. R. Townsend, Ph.D.
President, KTownsend Consulting
Committed to helping women live and lead...CONFIDENTLY!
www.DrKarenTownsend.com

Chapter 1

Something Bruised, Something Blessed

Nina Nicole

"But forget all that—it is nothing compared to what I am going to do. For I am about to do something new. See, I have already begun! Do you not see it? I will make a pathway through the wilderness. I will create rivers in the dry wasteland."

Isaiah 43:18-19, New Living Translation

I was terrified. Awakened by what I thought was my father's laughter, I tiptoed down the stairs to find out what was so funny. Standing in the doorway, I watched as my mother walked toward the chair in the middle of the kitchen, where my father told her to sit. After she sat down, I could tell she had been crying. Before I could rush over to wipe her tears, I was stopped in my tracks. My tired eyes zeroed in on his hands as he paced back and forth. They were huge. And from my vantage point, they were the embodiment of strength and protection. In this moment, however, I saw this larger-than-life hand raised high above his head—only to land across my mother's cheek.

Her screams pierced my soul.

Without thinking, I ran over and threw myself into her lap. Straddling her in the chair, I didn't know why he was hurting her, but I was sure he wouldn't hurt me. I was his sweetheart, a precious possession. So, I held on for dear life. I would protect her. Suddenly aware of my presence, he tried to loosen my grip. But I was determined. Clearly flustered, he gave up his efforts to pry me away. I was too strong. Ignoring our pleas for mercy, his rage was not deterred. He proceeded to strike every part of her body left exposed beneath my small five-year-old frame. So many questions filled my ribbon-adorned, pig-tailed head. *Who was this madman, and what had he done with my daddy? Why couldn't I make him stop? Why wasn't I enough?*

> *Why wasn't I enough?*

It wasn't the first time the officers stood on the other side of our front door. They had received *another* call about a domestic dispute. As I overheard my father weaving together an unjustifiable excuse for his behavior, I could also hear the other officer presenting mother with a choice. Standing there with a busted lip and blackened eye, she was sick and tired of being sick and tired. The look in her eyes told me that the decision had been made.

It was time to be free.

We only had time to gather a few items before we left the red brick townhome for the last time. We slid into the backseat of the police cruiser and waited, with uncertain anticipation, to be transported to the safety of a battered women's shelter in an undisclosed location.

There were no hugs and kisses.

I didn't even get to say goodbye.

After many days, and long, sleepless nights in the confines of a community room slightly partitioned by a chest-of-drawers here or there, my mother got the keys to our new home. My excitement turned to sadness because I knew my father wouldn't be there. As I grew older, it was hard to let go of him. It was hard to be without his sporadic presence; to love and not hate him. Though there were lingering thoughts of his terrorizing rage, I couldn't do it. I *wouldn't*.

He was my dad. No matter what was visible to the world, my spirit told a different story.

Don't get me wrong. I often walked about with a heavy heart because mine was the dad that was known by some as a hustler, jailbird, womanizer or abuser. He wasn't there for most milestones, birthdays or random Saturday afternoons. But he was still the keeper of my heart, and no one could take his place. Not even as I recall the first time that I stood in the glow of flashing red and blue lights. My eyes witnessing bags of crack cocaine being emptied from his pockets. Not even when the officer struggled to close the metal handcuffs around his bulky wrists. And not even when I felt the weight of his sulking profile sitting in the paddy wagon as I watched it drive by...downtrodden and defeated. In retrospect, the scene was quite powerful. I was able to see him, finally, as a child of God. One who, like me, had made mistakes, failed to resist temptations, and needed forgiveness more times than a few.

> *He wasn't there for most milestones, birthdays or random Saturday afternoons.*

So, I longed for the misfortune of being subjected to invasive pat downs from guards from one prison to the next; a subjection that paled in comparison to my reward: closely monitored quality time. Even in such despicable surroundings, he shared the Word of God. I learned to love and honor him without condition or unachievable expectations.

He was who he was—still my father—and I was still his sweetheart. Behind those bars, I had his attention and he had mine. With every time-sensitive, prepaid, institutionally monitored call, that attention was loving and undivided. I hung onto every God-anointed word.

Even though the vision of love I carried from these surroundings was quite skewed, I still had hope. I heard fairytales in the shadows of great elders past. Honorable, God-fearing men. The love, honor and respect shown to their wives, humble women of God, true protectors and providers. But I wondered if they were figments of my imagination. Since I had never encountered such a man, the image was fading.

So, I hid under this illusion of provision and protection. But beneath this clouded headspace was the reality of my father's violent outbursts, random women and unpredictable bouts of absence. Living a fantasized truth, I couldn't find myself. I never felt secure. And with dysfunctional ease, I blended my reality with the illusion. In his presence, I was persistent, but unsure. In his absence, he was a dream that I chased. And like many, I went looking for him in all the wrong places. Wandering aimlessly, I wondered when my first love, or anything like it, would ever come around again.

Big Girl Lost

Days after my eighteenth birthday, sitting behind a small, uncluttered desk, my doctor looked me in the eyes over the rim of his glasses as he said, "I'm sorry. You will not be able to have children." He explained that the pain I'd been experiencing over the years was because I had Endometriosis. My tubes were blocked with scar tissue, making it impossible to conceive. The proof had been captured through the lens of a tiny scope he inserted into my abdomen a few weeks before, a copy of the footage provided for later viewing displeasure. I was focused on his lips for a while as he spoke. But I hadn't heard a thing, except that I was broken. *Less than a woman. Useless.* What man would want me now?

> *Living a fantasized truth, I couldn't find myself.*

My mother wanted a second opinion, a third if necessary. Crying hysterically, I burst through my grandmother's door and fell to her feet. She was my gateway to God. She would go to Him on my behalf because I didn't have a clue. My faithless attitude and wayward thoughts couldn't comprehend the bigger picture or God's timing. I wanted her to tell me why God didn't want me to be a mother. Why, when so many other people had children to mistreat and leave unwanted? I wanted the truth. Still sobbing, she commanded me to get up. Disgruntled, I wiped my eyes so that I could search hers.

With great conviction, she said, "You have to wait on the Lord!" Nothing more, nothing less. *What kind of answer was that?* Again, I was speechless and confused. I couldn't understand her level of faith. Her response to my tragedy was useless.

I needed answers. The doctor had them all, and with documented proof. The trusted man in the starched lab coat had declared my womb barren, and that was that. But all wasn't lost. I was officially grown. I'd do only what felt good and live without regret. My 'womanhood'; however, had given me a deceiving tap on the shoulder. I was nothing more than a little girl hiding within the shell of a woman. I didn't know what I didn't know. I had much growing to do.

> *I'm sorry. You will not be able to have children.*

Wreaking of confusion, a year later, I still couldn't see the forest for the trees. But that didn't deter my fixation. I was locked in. This twenty-one-year-old young man would rescue me from the vault of stored pain that was my mother's home. I saw what I wanted to see and ignored what I didn't. He was who he was, but I was going to make him what I *wanted* him to be, by any means necessary. He was all that my father was, and was *not*, but he wouldn't leave. I became a chameleon to serve him and earn his approval. This would make him stay. I kept praying for wedding bells that simply refused to ring. I kept praying for someone to call me "Mama". But my waiting seemed to be in vain.

For nearly seven years, I did just that. I waited for God to show up, like my grandmother said He would. Hanging on to my last thread of sanity, I was barely able to function. There were days when I begged God to put strength in my legs. It was all I could do to put on a happy face. I forgot how to hope. To me, it was a painful concept that was always followed by deep disappointment. I never grew bitter. I simply carried the weight of a broken heart. With blows to my soul, one after another, I was breathless.

We had robbed Peter and had no idea how to pay Paul. Both of us were out of work and the bills continued to pile. With shut-off notices and foreclosure looming, we were broke. Early one morning, I sat on the edge of the bed, deep in thought, but devoid of all hope. I was fatigued. An emptiness like I'd never felt came over me. Before long, I found myself clinging to my pillow. My face drenched in tears, I cried myself into a deep sleep. Three hours passed before I opened my eyes. I was completely famished. One medium pepperoni pizza, a pint of ice cream and a bag of chips later, I realized that something was *off*. I became conscious of the tenderness in my breasts and the fullness around my waist. While my mind was swimming in despair, my body was trying to tell me something.

Although I didn't openly display the pain of not being able to bear children, I never forgot the doctor's words. His prognosis was the only birth control we had ever considered. There would be no

> *He was all that my father was, and was not, but he wouldn't leave.*

babies. For years, this method had been foolproof. He did, however, warn us of the possibility of a life-threatening ectopic pregnancy. With all the symptoms in motion, I made my way to a free clinic and waited for the nurse to give me the verdict. Lost in a sea of childbirth pamphlets and uterine diagrams plastered over the walls, I didn't see the nurse as she stood beside me grinning from ear to ear.

"Congratulations!" flowed with sincere joy from her mouth.

It was short-lived as she listened to me explain my diagnosis. I was scheduled for an ultrasound the next day. This was a medical emergency, and I didn't want to die. Moreover, I didn't want to get attached to this empty dream.

I had come to terms with my childless fate; however, I noticed a stirring in my soul I couldn't quite explain. I looked for confirmation that the dot on the screen was a baby, trapped in my tubes, that would never make it out of my womb. But it was a confirmation I wouldn't receive. There'd be no surgery to remove the fetus. Instead, we made appointments for prenatal care. My head was spinning circles around my heart. The doctor had said, "No." But grandmother said, "Wait."

God showed me that He was the true author of my fate. I would be a mother, and they would call me blessed.

The fire inside me took on a life of its own. Jesus was real, and I was going to tell anyone who'd listen. This beautiful black child was my son. A child who, by medical standards, never stood a chance. Defying all scientific odds, my son would be born, proving that science is at the mercy of God. He was a special delivery who allowed me to experience God for myself. He was my living, breathing testimony.

Our son was healthy and happy, and we were gainfully employed. There was more laughter than tears, and things seemed to be looking up. Surely, he'd finally request my hand in marriage. But there was still a resistance lingering behind the love he had for me. Not one of conscious malice, but one of uncertainty. There was no guidance on the direction of our next steps. He made no secret of his indifference to holy matrimony; yet, I pushed. My friends were getting married and having children. They were going to church and living their best lives. *When would it be my turn? Why wouldn't God fix him? Why wouldn't He fix us?* I no longer wished to be the prize cow, serving up free milk by the gallon. I had prayed and got my answer. I was putting my foot down and he would see things my way. I was tired of playing this grossly distorted game of 'house'.

Pastor was thrilled to pencil us in for one random Saturday morning to officiate our ceremony. With only a week to work with, my 'wedding' was going to go off without a hitch. I was ready with my $60 off-white suit, borrowed bouquet and tiara from Walmart. But with my father sitting in prison two hours away, it was my brother who gave me away. At the end of that aisle, I was finally married before God, my son, and about a dozen witnesses.

I had everything I wanted, in *pictures* and on *paper*. But as life would have it, pain, disappointment and regret managed to set up shop and acquire permanent residence in our humble abode. I cried like I did when my dad would leave. Without words, my tears begged him to stay. That would break him down, and sometimes, I'd have my way. But usually, my wet cheeks, puffy eyes and runny nose had no bearing upon whatever temptation lured my husband away. I wasn't daddy's sweetheart anymore. Neither was I this man's wife. I was replaceable. Rejected once again. Vulnerable, afraid and abandoned.

A never-ending cycle of immature, reckless, trauma-induced behavior led to the demise of our co-dependent relationship. While it was a marriage, as the laws of the land would tell, there was no sufficient promise between man, woman and God. I had no clear vision of what it meant to be a wife, nor did he know what the role of a husband truly entailed. This, however, wasn't entirely his fault. For almost twenty years, he could never truly live up to my misdirected expectations. Oddly enough, I expected more from him than I did myself. Even after all was said, and much left undone, I hadn't completely realized my own delusion. I subconsciously charged the task to this innocent man. He was to be my father, my savior. He was supposed to be my god. An impossible feat! But shame on him for being anything less. I'd be remiss to say he hadn't tried. Me and all my previously accumulated luggage was his to carry, along with his own. For that, I say, "Shame on me." My healing wasn't his responsibility.

A Time for Healing

As much as I tried to convince myself otherwise, the idea of 'healing', and the fundamental need for it, was foreign to me. I figured out that *just pushing through* wasn't healing. Simply bouncing back wasn't it either. Incessant inner struggles told a different story for as long as I could remember. It's difficult to keep your heart open after being stretched to traumatizing emotional limits. Although the scars remained, there had to be a remedy that would prevent their sting from rendering the same level of pain. I

> *I simply carried the weight of a broken heart.*

knew I had to be receptive to healing so I could finally grow. I had to make this commitment to myself.

I had to repent and ask forgiveness for my sins, both known and unknown. This search of my soul was more than a notion, proving to be a challenge like no other. In fact, I'd spent so much time working to forgive others that I didn't realize the need to forgive myself. I was used to being everyone else's victim. Besides, all I ever did was show them love, honor and respect to prove my loyalty. Yet, in return, all

I got was abuse and a dysfunctional bond. But I had set the stage. I trusted my unstable plans and manipulations to reincarnate my distorted vision of love. God's true blessings, well within reach, were an afterthought. I didn't know which way was up.

Months later, I attended a women's conference. I told myself there was no way I was going anywhere at 6 a.m. on a Saturday. But when the day arrived, I needed a message from God. When I entered the sanctuary, I saw hundreds of women, praising and worshiping God. I had never seen or felt anything like it. I wanted more. Soon, the pang from my spiritual famine was quelled. My thirst for knowledge grew. I knew God for myself. I knew I would never be the same, and frankly, I didn't want to be.

We've heard that God has a sense of humor. But my choice to abstain from sex was far from a joke. Laced with whirlwind romances, bouts of infatuation, and the benefits of 'special' friends, much time after my divorce was spent on a battlefield of unresolved fear and insecurity. It became painfully clear that my life depended upon a change. I needed to cleanse my mind, soul and body. Celibacy was the farthest thing from my mind. I couldn't give up my 'trusty' carnal crutch. Luring me time and again into unbridled lust, instant gratification and temporary satisfaction, it was my 'bandage' of choice. Consequently, the wounds that remained couldn't heal. They needed time to air out.

I was ready to clean house. The debris from the past had no place in my future. So, for five years, I abstained. What I wanted was a love that was pure and devoid of empty lust, one that was free of ties to my soul. No strings attached to anyone or anything not sent by God. Along with the impromptu flashbacks of untamed escapades were the tangible reminders that also needed to go. The thigh-high boots, paired with some racy lingerie, I tossed out. I realized that each item, thought and fleeting sensation were all attachments, deterring me from my true love. So, I purged. I owed it to myself and to my future husband. But more importantly, I understood that God required it.

> *I figured out that just pushing through wasn't healing.*

My Mama told me to be specific in my prayers. So, I dug deep. No more charades or trips to the build-a-man store, shopping through the lens of my flesh. The time for fun and games had come to an end. What I longed for was a man whose heart was after God, whom I could graciously follow into wedded bliss. Like the Bible said, I would "write the vision, and make my request plain" before God. Then, I'd be like Ruth: minding my business and serving the Lord. At the appointed time, this man, who had submitted to God, would find me.

Through a mutual friend, we became acquainted. It started with a conversation about love. More specifically, 1 Corinthians 13:4. He gave me his account of love as described by God and how he applied the Scripture to himself, both as a meditation and an affirmation. I was immediately in awe of his knowledge of God and this new approach to love. Although I didn't know it at the time, this introduction was in divine order.

Our courtship, which seemed to be a two-year biblical construction of an impenetrable foundation, invited us into the covenant between man, woman and God. I had another chance, and my prayers were answered. My man, sent straight from above, awaited me at the altar. I was in awe of the results of my faith. There was a peaceful stillness in the room. It was the assurance that all things had come together for the good because, in agreement, we loved the Lord.

Considering all of the prayer and sacrifice, you couldn't tell me I didn't have this marriage thing all figured out. I had finally arrived at the gateway to pure, holy matrimony. Sure, I knew everything wouldn't be peaches and cream. But I decided I could still control the outcome with a new approach and perspective. Then, without warning, reality bit me on my bare behind. Bills accumulating, work hours extended, parents ailing, and a child riding my last nerve, life was indeed happening. But since I knew better, I would *do* better. But *knowing* is only half the battle. *Doing*, on the other hand, is a never-ending spiritual spar.

> *I was in awe of the results of my faith.*

I thought I had grown tired of wearing the pants. Though I already had plenty of hats and ensembles to wear, I couldn't seem to take off those pants from last season! Caught up in a semi-forced, independent reality, I was convinced that all I could depend on was *myself*. Even if I failed, I was still in control. Though it's an admirable trait, I took independence to the extreme. So again, my pattern unfolded. I believed in God but refused to let Him take the wheel *completely*.

I stood firm, yet uncomfortably, in my husband's lane, unwilling and too afraid to budge. He was the head, but I didn't allow him to lead. True submission wasn't on the agenda. It was a familiar desperation presenting itself in a different form. Anxiety consumed me whenever he didn't let me dominate each task, decision and circumstance. It's no wonder I was so exhausted. Being submissive, I learned, is a daily challenge. And it's been my greatest hurdle thus far. God had sent him to give me rest, but I couldn't let go.

He became my biggest distraction. I was determined to do everything right this time, with all the tools and immovable faith. But after saying, "I do" *again*, I didn't realize how I'd managed to alienate God. Knowing better, I still placed my husband before God. Acting out of emotion, I tried to cater to his every whim. I tried to be everything, up to and including God. All the while, I was convinced I was acting in His will. After all, I was his helpmate and especially empowered with my super woman cape in tow. But I'd soon learn that my best would never be good enough without God at the center.

On occasion, "for better" may become "for bad." But, brace yourself. Before you know it, the bad takes an abrupt turn for the worse. When tensions are high, your mind can draw you into a rabbit hole of despair or even silent rage. Giving in to my emotions in lieu of seeking God and wise counsel, I reacted in response to pain instead of love. Submerged in my feelings, I was never sure whether to fight or take flight. Even when you're reminded of your hopes and dreams, and your vows, in times like this …obedience is *hard*!

Butterflies and roses are not the scene I wish to convey. I want you to know the truth. The conviction of your vows will surely test your faith, but perfection isn't the goal. Besides, who is perfect but God? So maybe you aren't a five-star chef. Your hair and nails aren't always slayed. Your home...less than immaculate. You'll never be the perfect anything, and neither will your husband. He won't always say the right thing, go above and beyond, or remain the hopeless romantic that never failed to make you blush. Also, beware that your mouth can tear down your home faster than your hands ever could. The power of life and death is in the tongue, so choose words wisely. I became mindful of offense and learned that everything didn't need to be said. In other words, think before you speak. Fix your mouth to pray *first*! It wasn't as complicated as I made it out to be. It's when you're alone with your thoughts in a room full of people. It's when your head is about to explode as your husband tests your patience. Before layers of stifled feelings and unspoken choice words form to leave your unfiltered lips, talk to God and seek Him. Use prayer to nurture the foundation upon which your union was built. As a wife, know that there is power in your prayers. Own it!

At last, consider this, be the love you seek. When your blood reaches its boiling point, know that love is patient. Refrain from tearing down in word or deed. Choose to be kind.

> *At last, consider this, be the love you seek.*

Be a bridge, not a tower. Love is not a competition. Share in accomplishment and knowledge. Don't boast or be filled with pride. Feelings and respect matter. Rudeness has no place in love. Consider compromise. Love doesn't press for its own way. Commit to trusting God to do something new, beyond all you can imagine. Remain calm. Irritability brings about misdirected strife. Put away the ledger of mistakes. Where there is love, there is resilience, faith and hope. Love never fails.

For more information about Nina Nicole and her fearless way of life, visit www.ninanicolebrown.com.

SELF-REFLECTION QUESTIONS

1. Describe what it was like when you began to have a personal relationship with God.

___

2. How does being fatherless show up in your life today?

___

SELF-REFLECTION QUESTIONS

3. What are the triggers blocking your healing?

___

4. When considering forgiving yourself or someone else for an offense, what are the benefits of forgiveness?

___

Chapter 2

To Have and To Hold Onto

Allison Retzlaff

"Whoever confesses that Jesus is the Son of God, God abides in him, and he in God. So we have come to know and to believe the love that God has for us. God is love, and whoever abides in love abides in God, and God abides in him."

1 John 4:15-16, English Standard Version

"I don't think you know who your dad is."

At twenty-eight years old, I sat on my parents' front porch with the man who had played the role of 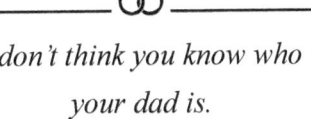 my stepdad for the past twenty-four years. We were talking about my childhood and mindsets. But when he spoke those words, he rocked me to the core. The truth in the statement was undeniable, and it was something I still walked in.

> *I don't think you know who your dad is.*

Growing up, I had three father figures. Having three father figures, to some, seems abundant; yet, I grew up not knowing who my dad really was. My biological father was always around. He was supportive as much as he could be with his mental disabilities. He always made big events like birthdays and holidays. He loved me and showed me love as much as he was capable. But he was never around for my everyday life.

My sister's dad took me in as his own. But when he filed for custody for my sister, I was abandoned because I wasn't his by blood. He and I were close. I considered him one of my best friends. He always reassured me that my blood meant nothing to him. I was his, regardless of blood. But when he got divorced and remarried, he changed. We fought, and on my way out of town I stopped by to reconcile our relationship. In that conversation, he brought up my blood, pointing out the fact that I wasn't his biologically. I ran out of there, watching him chase after my car in the rearview mirror. He never reached out to make things right, and I never did either. To this day, we don't have a relationship.

Last, but not least, is my stepfather. That's the man I lived with since I was four years old. He loves me in his own way. When he made that statement to me on the front porch, he was questioning why I never thought he loved me as his own. In that moment, all I could think about was all the times he made sure I knew he *wasn't* my daddy. I felt unclaimed, unloved, abandoned, rejected, worthless. I felt like a failure. A failure as a human to be loved by a father. Nobody wanted me. The love I experienced was conditional. There was no safety in mistakes. If you messed up, it just meant more love lost. I didn't earn love.

> *Being raised in a split family isn't easy.*

Being raised in a split family isn't easy. A lot of the time, it was miserable. My mom was a single mother for the first four years of my life. She was the epitome of a hard worker. Her story amazes me because it speaks nothing but resilience, strength and determination. The life that she has built inspires and pushes me to be better. When I was four, my mom started dating the man she married ten years later. About the same time, according to my mom, this is when my sister started refusing to go with her dad on the weekends without me. So, he agreed to take me too. From that point on, he became my dad. It was someone for me to claim, and I had someone who claimed me. I was with him every other weekend and most of the summer. His family took me in as one of their own too. There was no separation. Their family was my family.

As my sister and I got older, we started sharing things we were experiencing at home. We expressed how it felt being raised to behave through fear rather than love. Her dad didn't feel that it was a healthy environment for us to be raised in. This was the first time my blood came into play. During my seventh-grade year, he filed for custody of my sister. When he did that, everything changed. I was no longer allowed to go with him. He was forcefully no longer my dad. Every other weekend after that, I'd watch my sister leave while I was left behind. Every summer, I said "Goodbye," knowing I was being kept from the people I knew as family. I felt unloved and unwanted. I felt trapped and broken. I felt fatherless. I was always longing to reconcile, but I had no control in the situation. That was until my senior year.

As I got older, things in my home got worse. My relationship with my mom and stepdad was in shambles. Although my mom is one of my best friends now, that wasn't always our story. When I was a senior in high school, I started sticking up for myself. My mom and I fought weekly. Then, she would kick me out. I came home Sunday night after being gone all weekend. I went to school for the week, to only end up doing the same thing all over again. This continued routinely for a month or so, until I came home one Sunday and we had another huge fight. It was the straw that broke the camel's back. I declared that I was done. I refused to stay in the cycle. I was officially leaving home. This time, I wouldn't be back. I left. Even then, God was with me.

I ended up staying with a woman I had met only months before. I had spent a few hours with her every week while I volunteered in the community. She was my lifesaver. She and her family took me in, provided for me, got me a phone, shuttled me to school every day, and set me up for prom and graduation. All of which I could never repay. I was given a phone, so I was able to be in contact with my sister's dad again. I'm sure he was one of my first calls. I was determined to have my relationship back with the man I called Dad. When we reconnected, we both cried. He shared how hurt he had been the past several years, not being able to see me or talk to me. He told me my blood never mattered to him. I was his. He told me how sorry he was to have missed all of our time together. It was all that I needed. It was the reassurance that I longed for. I was claimed.

I planned on moving to Indiana when I turned eighteen that August. I couldn't wait to finally live out the life I'd dreamed of having. That's not to say that I didn't have a good life with my mom and stepdad. But I couldn't see or accept the love they had to give at the time. When I moved up there in August, he started to teach me to be an adult and how to survive in this world. He immediately worked to get me a license and a job. When I got a job, he taught me how to manage my money. He also bought me my first car. He made sure that I learned responsibility by having me pay for half of the bills, and by teaching me the importance of making them on time. I felt cared for. All was right, but I was young and naïve. This is where my first serious boyfriend entered the story.

I ended up moving in with him, and it was wild. When we split up the first time, I was welcomed back home. It had shifted a little. I was now paying toward groceries and I was expected to pitch in more around the house. A few months later, I ended up back with my boyfriend.

A few months after, he broke up with me and kicked me out of his home. This time, I wasn't

> *She was a light in the darkness, hope and my rock.*

allowed back at my sister's dad's house. At the age of nineteen, I had no place to go. I was about to be homeless. I called my mom and she talked to my aunt. Next thing I knew, I was moving in with her. I could write a whole book on who this woman was to me. In short, she was everything I needed. She was a light in the darkness, hope and my rock. She showed me what unconditional love looks like. She led me to Jesus. Her reflection of Him was too good to deny. She was never pushy, and she always saw me as good, even though she got a lot of bad. I was safe to make mistakes with her. She was truly how God removed the walls and lies of worthlessness, rejection and failure. She fought every single one of those lies with her kindness and love for me. It is something that has impacted my life forever.

The following year I gave my life to the Lord, and immediately jumped into serving His kingdom. I knew from the beginning that I would be in full-time ministry (though it's shaping out differently than I had planned). By the end of that year, my aunt became extremely ill. After months of taking it day by day, in hopes that she would make a positive turn, she didn't. My family and I finally convinced her to go to the hospital. We found out that she had stage four ovarian cancer. It was all over her abdomen. There was no hope. They gave her three to six months to live.

> *Her dying in my arms led me to believe that I didn't have enough faith to save her.*

I couldn't begin to describe the prayers that I prayed for that woman's healing. I had faith! I had complete faith that God would perform a miracle. She would be a living testament to His power. She came home and seemed to be getting worse. I was still believing God for a miracle though. I knew He could do it. On March 15, 2013, her legs gave out while I was moving her. We were sitting on her bedroom floor, having what would be our last conversation. She took her last breath on my shoulder. It is something I will never forget. It crushed me. Her dying in my arms led me to believe that I didn't have enough faith to save her. Yet again, this reaffirmed the belief that I was a failure in all things. This resulted in me running from God.

Running Away

I turned back to everything I knew before I met Jesus: drugs, sex, parties and a stagnant lifestyle. I wasn't growing forward in life anymore. I was stuck. Thank the Lord that He is a redeemer. Those years weren't wasted! They helped shape me into who I am today. They brought me to my husband. God showed me His faithfulness, who He is and who I am.

Jared and I met only a year into my running escapade. We worked together at a Hampton Inn, both on the front desk. I worked during the day and he worked at night. After a few months of working at the hotel, I found myself in a situation where I didn't have transportation to and from work. One of the blessings of working in a hotel is that it's full of rooms. I was able to stay in one; something I ended up doing for two years. During that time, Jared and I became close work friends. I ended up staying up all hours of the night with him, watching TV or YouTube videos, eating and talking. I was definitely interested from the beginning. Between his humor (including his dad jokes) and his witty charm, along with his beautiful blue eyes, I fell in love fast.

When I made it known that I was interested, he expressed that he just wanted to be friends. He didn't see me like that. We continued being friends and progressively started hanging out outside of the hotel. A couple of years into our friendship, Jared joined me at a party and spent the night with me. I was finally convinced that we had a breakthrough in our relationship. But then I went the whole day without hearing from him. I was scheduled to work and so was he. When he came in, he acted just as he would any other night. He didn't acknowledge a difference in the relationship, which was not okay for me. I called him out.

"If it's not going to go further, I don't want to continue being friends."

He informed me that his opinion of our relationship hadn't changed. We went the whole week without talking. That Friday, he called me and confessed his feelings for me, having me meet up with him. That night, we shared our first kiss, and it eventually led to more.

That year, Jesus was drawing me back to Him. After four years of running away, I decided to rededicate my life to Him. I hadn't had a relationship with Jesus since my aunt had passed away. As you may know, when He is welcomed into the mix, things have to change.

> *As you may know, when He is welcomed into the mix, things have to change.*

Jared and I were no longer on the same page in our relationship. We were living together at this time and deep in sin. He hated the sound of me praying or worshipping, to the point that he would come out of the room screaming at the top of his lungs. He didn't know Jesus and he had no plans of getting to know him. I cried out to God about Jared all the time. He shared with me that I was going to marry him and that he would be saved by Easter. That following Sunday, the greeter for the day at church stopped me and told me that she had a vision of me walking through the church doors with my husband, and that he would be there by Easter. Can you say confirmation? I bawled like a baby with joy and awe. I had a promise. With that promise, I could make it through anything. So, imagine my surprise when, a week later, Jesus told me that we need to break up.

I was convinced it was the enemy. There was no way I would receive that promise and confirmation, then be told to leave him. He didn't even have anyone in his life to speak truth and reflect Jesus to him! Jesus allowed our relationship to get so bad that the only thing I could do was leave. He put me in a position where I couldn't choose the relationship and choose Jesus at the same time. In that time, Jesus worked on us both. Jared received salvation and started coming to church a week before Easter, showing the faithfulness of God's promises. We didn't end up getting back together until July of that year. We were engaged to be married by that September. Now, we knew we would be together for the rest of our lives, but we didn't have a fairytale love. We had our disagreements and had them hard. The biggest ones were about money and our quality time together, or lack thereof. But we wrote these off for the most part. We got married and everything that had been an issue before marriage was magnified. That was when our problems truly took hold of us.

We were constantly at odds. We didn't honor each other, and love seemed hard to find. I just buried myself in work and tried to always be busy doing something to avoid contact that was sure to end in an argument. We got physical with each other on two different occasions, one of which led to the cops being called. This was so significant to me because I had been raised to defend myself. I always promised myself that I would never be in a relationship where someone put their hands on me. I am a strong woman who doesn't put up with that kind of thing. Jared was wrong for touching me in that manner. However, what happens when it's not just him, but it's me too? We were so broken. It was all because of his point of view toward me, or so I thought. Every argument we had, I pointed out how he could have handled a situation differently, and, in my opinion, better. He was never right. He needed to fix his heart because *he* was broken. He shared on multiple occasions that I didn't look good enough physically. He always said it in anger to stab me in my insecurities about my body, so it definitely hurt me. I remember crying out to God about my husband. I was a good person

I always promised myself that I would never be in a relationship where someone put their hands on me.

with a good heart. Why would God give me a husband who didn't want me, just like all of the other people in my life? He was supposed to be the one person who loved me when no one else did. He was supposed to reflect Jesus' love for me, and I wasn't getting any of it.

On top of that, we both wanted a family, a big one. After I turned twenty-seven, I was diagnosed with PCOS. It's a condition that affects my fertility and not in a good way. This just fed our problems. We tried for a year on medication, with no results. We were then referred to seek a fertility specialist. Eventually, we went to a doctor that was highly recommended by friends who suffered from the same condition. However, the results were the same. All we could do was trust God. Knowing that His timing is perfect, when it came time for our babies to come, nothing would stop God from forming them in my womb. The faith I had was feeling more and more like defeat. It was the cherry on top of all of our other problems.

Pursuing Patience

None of our issues were getting better. In the middle of us trying to conceive, we had started talking seriously about getting a divorce. We were losing the last drop of hope we had left. We argued almost

> *In the middle of us trying to conceive, we had started talking seriously about getting a divorce.*

every day. There was rarely ever peace or joy or love. Nothing but resentment and regret clouded our everyday life. After deciding to not seek medical help for a baby anymore, we had one argument too many. On a Wednesday night, we followed through with our previous discussions and my husband moved out and in with his parents. Coming home to that empty house was one of the worst feelings I've ever had. I didn't sleep in my bed for the rest of the week, opting to fall asleep on the couch with the TV on most times. Even with us living apart, and choosing to follow through with divorce, we couldn't stop talking to each other. During one of our conversations, we ended up arguing again.

"If you hadn't said that, we wouldn't be arguing," I said.

"Here we go again. I'm always the one to blame," he replied. He refused to entertain the conversation any further and hung up.

I immediately went to my room, sat on the bed and started crying. Everything was adding flames to the mess that was already burning. I cried out to God for help. At that moment, the Lord revealed that I wasn't listening to my husband. The Holy Spirit walked me through the conversation my husband and I had just had. The Holy Spirit showed me that it wasn't what my husband said, but rather how I received what he was saying that started the argument.

In John 9, you'll find the story of how Jesus performed a miracle and restored a beggar's eyesight. When the Pharisees heard, they brought the man before them and had him tell of his healing miracle. The Pharisees refused to believe it. They heard testimony from his parents, proving that this was in fact their child who was born blind. Still, this did not convince them. They had the man share his testimony again, and in the end, kicked him out of the synagogue, unable to believe that Jesus was good. The Pharisees had religious filters that didn't allow them to receive truth. As the Lord walked me through my argument with my husband, he showed me that I had been blinded by filters. Through these filters, I couldn't receive anything from my husband as he shared his heart.

He exposed the filters I was operating out of, including the filters that said I was worthless, unwanted and unloved. It made me react in a defensive manner. To this day, it is one of the most amazing things God has done for me. It is allowing me to walk in freedom and truth slowly, but surely.

When He gave me this revelation, everything shifted. I could now assess and operate differently. I was able to see how I had not been serving my husband or our house as a wife. I wasn't honoring him. We had lived in the house for almost four years, yet the home was nowhere near able to host company. The walls were even half painted. I started getting the house together.

I was determined to get my husband back. My husband was determined to stay away.

At the end of January, the church I was attending at the time was doing a fast. I took part, but it slipped my mind to pray to the Lord about what I needed during the fast. Two days before the fast was over, while driving to work, I cried out to God. I told Him I was believing for Him to restore my marriage. I knew it was only two days away, but I had the faith that He could do it. The day before, I told Jared not to call me anymore. It felt like I was on a roller coaster with him. I couldn't take the back and forth with our relationship. I knew if this happened, then it would be a miracle. In less than twenty-four hours, God answered my prayer, with Jared coming back home.

> *I was determined to get my husband back.*

We put ourselves on a one-week trial. If we could make it a week, then we had a chance. That's how bad things had gotten. We could literally base our hope off of a week of being around each other. It was a great week. He hasn't left since, and our relationship is so much better than it was before. Just in the shift of me not seeing and receiving through the filters, the change has been amazing. This is all still recent. We are still figuring it out, but now we can have tough conversations and sometimes arguments, without it feeling like the end of the relationship. We come up with solutions that fit us both. It just draws us into unity with one another. This would not have happened before. We could never reach a resolution in unity. I know we have a ways to go, but I don't dread it anymore. It brings me excitement and joy because I now have the confidence to know we are going to stick this thing out until the end. I know that I am chosen, I am loved, and I am claimed.

We are now married to a new way. We have hope again! Along with communication and commitment, to maintain being married in a new way, I have taken a few steps. When Jesus revealed my filters to me, I realized I had trauma and hurt that was feeding them. Step one was me seeking professional help to walk through healing those wounds. Another step was fixing my eyes on Jesus.

As previously mentioned, in John 9, the Lord exposed filters to me. It also spoke to fixing my eyes on Him and His character. In verses 30-33, the beggar challenged the Pharisees with God's truth and His character to show that Jesus was of God. Instead, because their eyes were fixed on their laws and

> *Step one was me seeking professional help to walk through healing those wounds.*

practices versus God, they were unable to accept what the beggar was saying. This shows that if we have eyes fixed on God, and who He is, we will be open to receiving truth, even if it goes against our beliefs or traditions. By fixing my eyes on Him, I grew in intimacy with God.

He showed me that I didn't have the firmest of foundations, but that He was washing away the sand and filling it with His truth. I am starting to finally walk in freedom and the fullness of all that He has for me.

While my fatherly relationships aren't perfect, I can see changes as God works to redeem them. As He replaces my filters that I have been operating out of with His filter of love, I am able to see them and our relationships in a different light. He reminds me of how much He loves them. If He is in me, then I have the capacity to love them like that too. This filter is also what is allowing me to have a different view toward my marriage and my husband, making all the difference.

In seeing the changes in my personal life, He has given me a passion to see others walk in freedom through love, as well. Currently, I am in the process of starting a non-profit focused on outreach, community and discipleship called Arise Cincinnati. Through Arise Cincinnati, we are creating a curriculum called *Firm Foundation* that will teach individuals how to have a personal intimate relationship with Jesus, making Him their firm foundation. This is what has made the biggest difference in my life, coming to know Jesus intimately and allowing Him to be the rock on which I stand. This is my passion.

For more information about Allison and her fearless way of life, please visit www.arisecincinnati.com.

SELF-REFLECTION QUESTIONS

1. What personal or professional relationships do you see as broken and why?

_____

_____

_____

_____

_____

2. What kind of filters are you looking through currently?

_____

_____

_____

_____

_____

 SELF-REFLECTION QUESTIONS

3. If you were to put on the filter of God's love toward a person involved in a broken relationship with you, how does your view of them change?

___

4. What practices can you put in place to actively shift your filters to be God's filters?

___

Chapter 3

First Comes Love, Then Comes Rejection

Tenita C. Johnson

"For the LORD will not reject his people; he will never forsake his inheritance."

Psalm 94:14, New International Version

For a season, I forgot I didn't know him. For a while, the fact that I've never met my father didn't stop me from moving forward.

Then, I got married.

Ironically, my mother gave birth to me when she was only fourteen, which just so happened to be the age at which I met the man I know as my husband today. At the time, my then boyfriend was four years older than me, which sent my mother into lawyer and private investigator mode. She threatened to put him in jail for statutory rape. She immediately forced me to get the Norplant inserted into my arm since she didn't trust me not to have sex, let alone *safe sex*. At the time, that form of birth control was effective for five years. It would at least prevent me from getting pregnant through my first year of college.

Little did I know, I was reliving my mother's past and pain—and her worst nightmare—right before her very eyes.

Rumor has it that my father was also several years older than she was when she gave birth to me at fourteen years old. Based on the stories I've heard over the years, my five uncles and grandfather ran him out of Chicago to another state, which further adds to the reason I've never met him. I've never talked to him on the phone or via video. There's never been any special delivery from dad on my

> *There's never been any special delivery from dad on my birthday or Christmas morning.*

birthday or Christmas morning. Many people say, "You don't miss your water until your well runs dry." I beg to differ. For me, the well has always been dry, dark and non-existent. Yet, there's a void in my life that is too large to explain in natural words.

Because my father didn't stay with her, when it came to Jermaine, my mother always told me, "He's not going to marry you!"

"He's using you! Can't you see that he has other women?"

"If he gives you $150, he will want $150 worth of your time and sex!"

Through the lens of her own pain and past mistakes, she knew exactly how my story would play out. *Or so she thought.*

After years of promiscuity, identity crises and depression, I'd accepted Christ at the age of twenty in Paris, Missouri at Faith Walk Ministries while attending the University of Missouri-Columbia. One of my college friends always made it clear that if she went to the club with me Saturday night, I had to go to church with her on Sunday, no matter how tired I was. As you can see, eventually she won.

By the time I was twenty-four, I not only found myself pregnant with twins, but I found myself engaged to the love of my life whom many said would never marry me. I didn't know it then, but that was the beginning of what has become a lifelong journey of healing much of what lied dormant for years. Even though I was saved and committed to living life for Christ, I wasn't healed. I wasn't delivered. There was still much work to be done.

> *Even though I was saved and committed to living life for Christ, I wasn't healed.*

The Reflection

Without my permission, my marriage became a mirror—magnifying all the flaws and broken places I'd swept under the rug for too many years to count. While many bask in marital bliss for months, if not years, after they say, "I do!", I found myself in a deep depression immediately. Maybe the loss of twins the day after we were wed played a huge part in my day-to-day emotions. But something larger was brewing beneath the surface.

A year after we lost the twins, I gave birth to Xavier Zachariah. We were also raising my husband's son from another relationship. He was seven years old when we married, so we had an eight-year-old and an infant. For weeks, I "woke up on the wrong side of the bed." When my husband or children said, "Good morning!" or "Good night!" I didn't know how to respond to that. Furthermore, many days, I didn't *want* to respond to that. I didn't grow up in a house hearing either of those things. My husband used to tell me, "You're not happy! You need counseling!"

Those aren't the words any new bride wants to hear. After all, it wasn't my fault that I was broken. But it wasn't my husband's or my children's fault, either. At the time that we married, I was twenty-four and my husband was traveling 95% of the time. So, after a brief break after the wedding and the sudden loss of the twins, he hit the road again—leaving me to raise his seven-year-old son he'd had with another woman while in the military. Although I'd married the love of my life, I didn't think I'd signed up for everything that came with that love. What started out as him traveling Monday through Friday, with weekends at home, soon turned into working overtime in another state on certain weekends. Eventually, my husband was working on a project out of state for three weeks, including weekends. Talking on the phone wasn't enough. I hit my breaking point—and we'd only been married about six months.

> *After all, it wasn't my fault that I was broken.*

"Look, I didn't sign up for this. I think we should get a divorce," I said.

"What do you mean a divorce?" he asked, preparing to finally come home from this three-week extended assignment. "I have to work!"

"I don't want to be a part of a long-distance marriage. You leave me here for weeks to raise *your* son while you get to hop on and off planes every week. This isn't what I imagined this to be at all."

Even though there were several key players to consider in the equation of the family, at the time, it was all about *me*. *My* wants. *My* needs. *My* pain. *My* hurt. *My* comfort. And when that picture didn't fit perfectly into the frame in which I'd envisioned in my mind, I was ready to get out of the boat—even though I didn't know how to swim, nor did I have a life jacket.

Before I could make plans to silently divorce my husband and move out of state, he did what many

> *My wants. My needs. My pain. My hurt. My comfort.*

people in my life have never done: *he chose me*. That weekend, upon his return, he quit his job and began the search for a new position that didn't require traveling. In the moment, I felt like that was the stupidest thing he could have done. We were newly married and planning to buy a house. We both had mountains of debt. We were raising a seven-year-old, whose biological mother didn't offer any financial support, and we were still paying off the wedding. He couldn't have picked a worse time to quit his job.

In hindsight, the fact that he quit immediately, without a plan B or C, spoke volumes to the fact that he was willing to put his marriage and family *first*. I'd been chosen and hand-selected for a few things in life before marriage, but I never felt *first*. I didn't even know how to stand in the position of being *first* in anyone's life, let alone my husband's. My father had clearly chosen something or someone other than me as *first*. Even though I'm the only child, my mother was forced to *make me first* simply because "it was the right thing to do" or because it made her look like a "good parent". By her words and her actions, it was crystal clear that she didn't *choose* me first. My mother reminded me often that she couldn't have birthday gifts or Christmas presents because she had me. She reminded me that I should be grateful for anything anyone ever gave me because people only did nice things for me because I was her child, not because they loved me individually. Subconsciously, I became accustomed to simply being tolerated, not celebrated.

I oftentimes came in last or second to last at my track and cross country meets, long after fans for the other students had left the stands. It hadn't dawned on me then. But I'd become so accustomed to being tolerated instead of celebrated, so accustomed to being last, that I didn't even feel comfortable accepting the place of *first*.

When my husband told me, "You look good!" or "You're beautiful!" my response wasn't, "Thank you!" It felt weird and ingenuine. It felt fake. I didn't know how to receive a compliment like that when, for more than twenty years, I hadn't heard anything like it. Since I

> *If no one told me I was beautiful or pretty, that had to mean I was ugly.*

hadn't heard those words from family, friends or even boys my age, I assumed the opposite was true. If no one told me I was beautiful or pretty, that had to mean I was ugly. That's the story I told myself for years silently. And it was rearing its ugly head in my marriage. I didn't know what to call it at first. I couldn't put my finger on it or give it a name at the age of twenty-five, twenty-eight or even thirty years old.

Today, I recognize this infection as the *root of rejection*.

Like any other infection in your natural body, if left untreated, it will spread—as it did in my marriage.

By the time we'd been married for three years, we'd considered divorce too many times to count. The bottom line was I was a twenty-seven-year-old who wasn't *happy*. And it had nothing to do with my husband. I wasn't happy on the inside, so it didn't matter what those who loved me did for me on the outside. I didn't have joy. I didn't have peace. After the loss of the twins, I was always afraid that every child I became pregnant with after them would die. Because my husband had threatened to leave so many times, and my father had *never* been present, I was afraid that it was only a matter of time before my husband left me forever. Since he was raised by a single mother as well, he had also threatened to take my children with him when he divorced me. Even though we had some great moments in our marriage early on, they were often overshadowed by the dark times that seemed to last ten times longer.

My husband loves to cook and, many times, he would fix my plate for me and bring it to me wherever I was in the house. Instead of me appreciating this random act of kindness, I was more irritated. He often brought me my plate at inconvenient times, like when I was just getting out of the shower or when I was preparing to get on a virtual training and didn't have time to eat. He also showered me with gifts, like Michael Kors bags, Cole Haan shoes and dress boots for my birthday or Christmas—but none of those things made me happy or brought me joy. After seven years of going around the same mountain, I realized I had to get some professional help. At that point in life, I had to come face to face with the harsh reality that we didn't need marital counseling. This wasn't a broken marriage issue.

I needed individual counseling. This was a broken me issue.

I hired a male counselor at our church, who was familiar with me and Jermaine's story. We met every other week for a couple of years. We seemed to be peeling back the layers of damage slowly but surely. However, it wasn't enough to prevent the negative words we'd spoken over our marriage for years from manifesting.

In one of the seasons of our marriage where we didn't speak to each other for weeks at a time, he gave me an ultimatum. I was preparing to travel to Chicago for my cousin's graduation. While there for only a weekend, my husband wanted me to decide whether or not this marriage was truly something

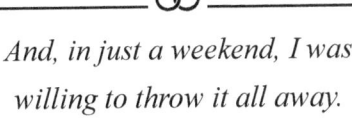

And, in just a weekend, I was willing to throw it all away.

I wanted. Although I had many warnings, many red flags, I found myself having a one-night stand with a man whom I'd known since childhood. In my mind, the marriage was over. We'd talked about leaving so much that I felt like I had one foot already out the door. We'd went so many days and weeks without speaking, so many nights without lying next to each other in bed, that I was pretty certain this was the end. And, in just a weekend, I was willing to throw it all away. I couldn't see any future or hope for a better marriage than what we'd always had. I was thirty-four. We'd been married for ten years. But life didn't seem to be getting any better.

But as He always does, God had other plans for what appeared to be my greatest downfall. The Holy Spirit convicted me to tell him about the affair when I came home. Terrified, shaking and trembling, I told him at our home church on a Friday night in a classroom, alongside my counselor at the time, Rick Thues. I'll never forget the way Jermaine stormed out of the church doors and burned rubber leaving the church parking lot, while I sat with Rick, trying to get a plan of action for my life moving forward. It was over. The years of unhappiness, unworthiness, depression and sadness were suddenly *done*.

Perfected Love

By Saturday morning, Jermaine had packed most of the house and stacked boxes and tubs in the living room. We had never got this far before in our divorce process. So, I knew this had to mean he was really done this time. This was the last straw.

But by Sunday morning, on Fathers' Day, he started asking questions. He wanted answers.

"What did he do that I don't?"

"What did he say to you that I haven't?"

"I'm willing to make it work if you show me what you need."

"The Lord showed me I've done some things that are much worse. Can we pray?"

I was floored. Flabbergasted. Confused. I didn't know any man who would stay with his wife after she'd not only had an affair, but also had the audacity to come and tell him to his face that she committed adultery. To make matters worse, three months later, we discovered I was pregnant with my daughter, Nyla. Of course, because of the affair, my husband was in an emotional tug of war. While he prayed that she was indeed his daughter, he didn't know if she was because of the affair. For nine months, he was on edge, wondering if the little girl he'd always hoped and wished for was indeed the child of another man. But when she was born, there was no doubt in his mind that she was his biological child.

Of course, because of the affair, my husband was in an emotional tug of war.

In the Word, 1 Corinthians 13:4-8 says, *Love is patient, love is kind. It does not envy, it does not boast, it is not proud. It does not dishonor others, it is not self-seeking, it is not easily angered, it keeps no record of wrongs. Love does not delight in evil but rejoices with the truth. It always protects, always trusts, always hopes, always perseveres. Love never fails.*

I was experiencing the epitome of love as God intended it to be and I didn't even know it. Because of the root of rejection, and fear of one more person leaving me, I was constantly subconsciously self-sabotaging. If I could leave him before he left me, it wouldn't feel like rejection. If I gave him a valid reason to leave me, like an affair, it wouldn't feel like rejection. Even if it did feel like rejection, it would feel *justified*.

For years, I tried to *justify* why my father wasn't in my life. It wasn't his fault. My family actually forced him to leave me and my mother. Maybe he was afraid they'd kill him since my mother was so young. Maybe he didn't know about me at all. He probably didn't know that I existed if my mother kept it a secret. Then, it would all make sense. Or maybe, he was unfit to be a father, so he felt like the best thing he could do for me was leave and not be a part of my life at all. No one told me these things. I didn't hear it from my father. But all of these justification phrases made me feel better than the raw reality of the thought, *"My father simply didn't want me and didn't want to be a part of my life."*

> *The truth was that I didn't love myself, so I couldn't possibly receive love from him.*

Unlike my father, my husband stayed. He stayed past the hurt and pain of rebuilding our marriage, knowing another man had slept with his wife. He stayed past the years of depression, suicidal thoughts, low self-esteem, selfishness and ungratefulness. The truth was that I didn't love myself, so I couldn't possibly receive love from him—or anyone else for that matter.

My healing journey from that point has been intense and intentional. I partnered with a counselor outside of the church, so I could get both the natural and spiritual perspective of the work I needed to do to heal at the core. I didn't just want to heal the symptoms; I wanted to get to the root of the matter and uproot the layers, one by one. The first method my counseling used to get to the root was called the Emotional Freedom Technique (also called EFT or Tapping).

I had weekly sessions with my counselor, a White female, for a year and a half, before we hit a roadblock in our belief systems. I hit a point in the healing process where I desired to be free from the addiction of masturbation and watching porn. She didn't see it as an addiction at all because many of her clients were using it as a means of release and it was "natural". It was clear she'd taken me as far as she could take me in the healing journey.

My next counselor was an African American female. Although she taught from spiritual principles, she was a licensed psychologist with her own practice. She was able to help me see things from a spiritual perspective, and also show me what I needed to do in the natural to continue the healing process. In addition to journaling and daily meditation, she gave me movies or TV shows to watch and evaluate. She told me what to eat and what not to eat to balance the energy levels in my body.

In addition, she enlisted me and my husband into a marriage bootcamp that she and her husband facilitated for couples around Michigan. The bootcamp was ten weeks long, for three and a half hours a week every Monday night. From communication, finances and forgiveness to intimacy and vision for the family, this bootcamp literally transformed our marriage from the inside out. More than that, it transformed the way we see our roles in the marriage and in the kingdom of God. We had to realize that we are not each other's enemy. There is an enemy, but we are not that enemy.

> *We had to realize that we are not each other's enemy.*

Today, me and my husband serve as leaders in that same marriage bootcamp, which has now grown nationally since we have the option to run it virtually. I'm still in counseling weekly. It's amazing that I've peeled back so many layers of issues and I've defined the root of many of those issues. However, uprooting 40+ years of baggage, much of which was passed on to me from the womb or even before, is a process. I wish I could wave a magic wand and totally get rid of the root of rejection. Rejection didn't take root overnight. Once rooted, its roots run deep though. I'm committed to continuing the healing process so I can bloom into the best version of me that God intended me to be.

Even when I'm not in a counseling session, I'm working to uproot rejection. Sometimes when my husband doesn't have sex with me, it's not because he's rejecting me. He's simply tired from a hard day's work. When he doesn't respond to my call or text immediately, it doesn't mean it's because he's with another woman or mad at me. He's simply busy at work. When he doesn't compliment me on a new outfit, new hairstyle or my makeup, it's not because he doesn't like it. Knowing my husband in the way I do now after eighteen years of marriage, I know he simply probably isn't paying attention, or his mind is focused on something else. I had to learn how to stop making everything about *me*. I had to stop viewing every response, or lack thereof, through the lens of rejection. I had to change my perception.

I'm also learning to stop looking for accolades and applause from others. Whether my husband or children compliment me or not, I know God calls me "fearfully and wonderfully made." I don't have less value or bring anything less to any table simply because others may not recognize my greatness. You have the ability to change the lens through which you view this thing called life. The choice is yours. Today, I have made a conscious decision to call out the root of rejection wherever or whenever it shows up in my life. In my journey of going from fatherless to fearless, I had to rehearse God's Word in Jeremiah 1:5 that says, *"Before I formed you in the womb, I knew you, before you were born, I set you apart; I appointed you as a prophet to the nations."*

> *I'm also learning to stop looking for accolades and applause from others.*

I am who God says I am. That is who I shall be.

For more information about Tenita and her fearless way of life, please visit www.soitiswritten.net.

SELF-REFLECTION QUESTIONS

1. Where does the root of rejection continually show up in your life?

2. What has been your personal experience with licensed counselors and what role do they play in your healing process?

SELF-REFLECTION QUESTIONS

3. If you are married, what things have been magnified in your life that need to be dealt with immediately, which you may not have recognized if you were single?

_____

_____

_____

_____

_____

4. What does the term "fearfully and wonderfully made" mean to you?

_____

_____

_____

_____

_____

Chapter 4

Divorcing the Monster of Trauma

Shameka Green

"If it be so, our God whom we serve is able to deliver us from the burning fiery furnace, and he will deliver us out of thine hand, O king."

Daniel 3:17, King James Version

At two years old, I became fatherless by default. My trauma was birthed the day my father died over a gold watch. I've heard many rumors about the night of his death. My father's family believes that my mother had a man rob and kill my father. I feel a lump in my throat every time I think my mother could be the reason that I'm fatherless. Trauma has robbed me of most of my early childhood memories. Google and old photos help me fill some voids in my story, but not all. The earliest memory I have is when I was six years old. When I look at the photos, I see a little, brown-skinned girl who adorns a smile on her face. I see a little girl with the loving nickname "Meme". Little Meme was the shy little girl with a Jheri curl, who loved Michael Jackson and New Kids on the Block. It seemed to be a good year for me.

> *My trauma was birthed the day my father died over a gold watch.*

It was the year my baby sister was born, and I finally had a playmate. Life was good, that was until trauma reared its ugly head. One day, I was sitting on my mother's bed, watching cartoons, when I heard a loud bang on the door. I jumped out of the bed and ran into our living room. When I turned the corner, I saw policemen everywhere. There were hours of chaos before we finally made it to my grandma's house. I kept asking my grandma where my momma was and why she wasn't home yet, but she wouldn't tell me the truth. Later that night, I overheard the true story when she was talking on the phone. My momma had been arrested for selling drugs. Life changed drastically for me that very moment.

> *The lack of stability made me feel like no one wanted me around.*

When my mother went to prison, my sister and I lived with my grandma for a short time, until she passed away from cancer. We were then moved from family member to family member. I went to so many elementary schools that I can't recall my childhood friends or graduation. The lack of stability made me feel like no one wanted me around. By the time I was entering into the sixth grade, my sister and I went to live with my father's sister. It's weird because we never talked about my father's side much. Yet, here we were, moving in with his sister. I'm not sure who made the decision, but no one asked me where I wanted to live. I was a stranger in the house of a relative I didn't know. Once an innocent shy little girl, I was now turning angry.

I never respected my aunt's rules, and she was slowly becoming tired of my mess. Within months, we were being shipped off to my momma's boyfriend's house. I didn't even know she had a boyfriend until we moved in with him. There were quite a few people living in that house, including his mother, Emma. Emma was sweet like a grandmother. She taught me how to bake cakes and she took me shopping for clothes. I had some good times there until trauma found me once again. Some memories are a blur, but the night of my abuse never left me. I was lying in bed when I heard the sound of the basement steps creek. My abuser made his way to the basement so we could "wrestle." He was supposed to be like a brother to me, my protector. But he didn't love me like a *sister*. The play fighting led to molestation.

After being robbed of my innocence, I felt numb. I just laid there. The abuse happened several times throughout my middle school years. I didn't have the heart to tell Emma because I wanted to stay with her. Living with Emma was the only sense of family or normalcy I had. Anger eventually got the best of me. The events that took place in that house created a monster inside me. My momma's boyfriend started treating me nastily.

He asked me questions like, "Are you having sex?" Then he'd say, "Let me see!" He pretended as if he was going to check between my legs. I hated this, and I never wanted to be alone with him. I started leaving the house for hours without telling anyone. Emma whooped me, but nothing seemed to work. Eventually, Emma took me to go live with my mother's brother.

I lost my smile. The once shy little girl was now a cold-hearted teen. While living with my uncle, I started sleeping with older guys to get attention and love. By the age of fourteen, I was pregnant. When I found out, I called Emma. I was nervous that I decided to tell her the news over the phone. She immediately told me I was having an abortion. She said, "You not going to ruin your life over some boy!" She immediately made me schedule an appointment and I was set to have an abortion. The day of the abortion was dreadful. People were protesting outside; showcasing poster boards with dead babies. Once we made our way past the protestors, there was no going back. I was instructed to make my way into the back to put my gown on. Once I laid on the examining room table, thoughts of the baby entered my head. I wondered if it was a boy or a girl. Those thoughts didn't matter because the decision was made for me. I figured Emma knew what was best for me, so I couldn't get attached to this baby. My young mind could not comprehend the fact that I was losing my first child.

After that day, I was no longer "Little Meme". In my head, I was a grown woman. The abortion didn't stop me from having sex. Living with my uncle gave me pure freedom to do whatever I wanted to do. I was enjoying this freedom until the end of my freshman year, when I found out my mother was coming home from prison. My mother called more and made plans for us to move in together. I hated it! I wanted to stay with my uncle and be free. During one of our phone conversations, my mother made plans for me to meet her "friend". I didn't want to get to know another friend or boyfriend. I couldn't

> *My trust level was low, and I was always unsure of a man's intentions.*

shake the uncomfortable memories from the last boyfriend. My trust level was low, and I was always unsure of a man's intentions. It took weeks before I agreed to meet my mother's new friend, Brent.

The man was determined to get to know me. He bought me gifts and brought me food. I was irritated every time he stopped by my uncle's house. Brent continued to visit me until my mother was released from prison. I believe his consistency probably helped me open up to him. At some point, Brent started living with us. At that time, we became even closer. I was beginning to experience the love of a father. I was starting to feel happy again, but for some reason, trauma made sure to visit me again. I was hanging out at my cousin's house when my pager started beeping nonstop. I didn't know the number, so I was hesitant to call back. When I finally called back, I heard my little sister's voice screaming through the phone. "Brent got shot!" Sadly, I remember this day like it was yesterday. My sister was with Brent when he was killed at a gas station. I never cried so hard in my life. The pain still lingers because we never found out who, what or why was behind his murder. What I know is that the love I always wanted from a father was gone.

Insecure Attachment

I felt numb for many years after Brent's death. My pain and abandonment led me back to chasing men. I never used drugs, but sex was definitely my addiction during my high school years. By the time I was nineteen, I was pregnant again. However, this pregnancy felt different. The thought of finally having someone to love was exciting for me. I was old enough to make my own decisions. I felt lucky because I had met what you would call the "good guy". El came from a vastly different background and his family was very stable. In my mind, El made the perfect father. The next year, I became a young mom. The life that I never could seem to have for myself, I wanted for my son. The early part of my 20s was spent being a mom and living with El. I was ready to be a wife, but he didn't want to be married. I expected my voids to be filled once I had a child and my own cute little family. But, that was not the case. I was still lonely inside. To cope, I went out to bars. One particular night, I met a man. We exchanged numbers and started talking on the phone almost every day. He told me he wanted to get married and have more kids. I was tired of feeling lonely and rejected. I wanted my dream family, so I decided to leave El.

> *I never used drugs, but sex was definitely my addiction during my high school years.*

I was head over hills deep into this new man's lies, which, of course, latched on to my illusions. I

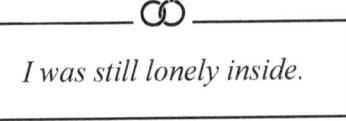

I was still lonely inside.

was unaware that I was marrying someone who was still battling with his own demons. At the time we met, he was on probation, which he continued to violate. Due to this, he spent several months in jail. In my head, he was going to be my husband. I created a happily-ever-after in my head. After several months of waiting for him, he was released from jail. As soon as we moved in together, I let him know that we had to get married. Things moved at rapid speed. I bought the rings, and we made plans to make it happen. We skipped the dating phase and went straight to marriage. I knew in my heart that I wanted to be a wife. At the time, I did not care to whom. But soon, I'd find out the detriment of my decision.

At the age of twenty-six, I finally became a wife. However, it was to a man I didn't know. My husband became extremely jealous and insecure. The jealousy turned into verbal abuse. The more he verbally abused me, the harder I tried to love him. Eventually, the verbal abuse led to physical abuse. I was in denial. I would downplay the abuse, as if we just had a little "fight." The cycle was always, "fight, then have makeup sex." All the makeup sex eventually led to me getting pregnant again. My marriage was rocky, to say the least. But I was excited about the new baby. I felt like this would make my marriage stronger. I wanted so badly to have that fairytale family, that I was willing to sacrifice myself in the process.

The fighting never stopped.

I lost the baby.

The miscarriage was devastating. I felt like my body was broken. I felt like I couldn't give my husband the child he wanted. The loss of our child intensified the arguments and we blamed each other. I never gave my body time to heal.

A few months later, I was pregnant *again*. In the beginning of this pregnancy, we both seemed so happy. My husband had a way of hiding his demons though. When I was about seven months pregnant, he accused me of cheating, and he beat me. The abuse eventually led to me being in the hospital. Yet, I was still in denial. I continued to convince myself that he loved me. I needed to make this work because he was part of my fairytale. I fed myself lies until my second son was born. After he was born, I saw a change in me. My physical appearance was changing. I didn't feel pretty, and I cried a lot. I slipped into depression.

Dark clouds seemed to loom over our house. The physical abuse never stopped. The makeup sex led to me getting pregnant *again*. I was already a mom of a six-year-old and an infant. My mother urged me to get an abortion. This time, I agreed. There was no way I could bring more kids into this mess. The day of my ultrasound, I found out I was pregnant with twins. Instantly, I had memories of my abortion at the age of fourteen. The painful memories of the abortion wouldn't allow me to kill my babies. God was sending me a double blessing, and I wasn't going to mess this up. I wanted my kids, but I was unsure about my marriage. The more I desired to make it work, the more it seemed as though God was leading me in another direction.

The dream of having a stable life seemed impossible. My husband often blamed our problems on staying in Detroit. He said the source of our problems was due to him not finding a job. We decided to pack up and move to Las Vegas. I moved on a whim with both my sons, while I was pregnant with twins. I just knew there would be a change. The city was bright and seemed to offer hope. God was planting a seed of hope in me, but it was not the one I expected. He does not give us what we want, but more of what we need. The cycle never stopped once we moved to Las Vegas. This marriage was not ordained by God. I remember the day I called out to God for help. I said a silent prayer, "God, I'm not strong enough to leave on my own. If this man is not for me, remove him." When you pray a prayer like that, you better be ready for the answer. Just a day or so later, my husband was arrested for stealing money from his job. He was eventually sent to prison. This was my opportunity for freedom.

> *The dream of having a stable life seemed impossible.*

We divorced, and by the age of thirty I was a single mom with four kids. This life was new to me, but God was waiting on me the whole time. I never really felt God's presence until my prayer was answered to leave my abusive marriage. I started going to church for the first time, because I was tired of my old ways. Drinking or sexing didn't make my problems go away. The fact that God saved me from mess was enough for me to surrender to God. I no longer depended on a man to make me happy. The only person I needed to lean on was God. My desire to seek God became stronger and stronger each week.

Love in a New Way

As a single mom, my mindset shifted. I dated for a short period of time, but it was never anything serious. Due to being molested, I refused to let any man meet my children. My walls were still up. El and I were doing a great job of co-parenting. We talked on the phone for hours like best friends. I enjoyed the company and conversations. The more we talked, the easier it was to let my guard down. During one of our phone conversations, we decided to give the relationship another try. He started flying to Las Vegas from Detroit to visit me and my children. My children loved him and gravitated toward him. At some point, the distance between us became unbearable. I was not interested in a temporary situation. If we were going to make this work, I knew he would need to move to Las Vegas, and we would need to be serious about marriage.

El agreed and made the move to Vegas. We were not living together long before we started ring shopping. I wanted a second chance at being a wife. I wanted a real family. We checked off all the 'boxes' to prepare for marriage, like pre-marital counseling at church. However, I still didn't understand what being a wife entailed. When happiness came, trauma always wanted to rob me of those moments. I wasn't prepared for the monster inside me to resurface. I'd gone from the perfect life to living a lie. We took family photos, and I put on this fake smile. If my husband didn't touch me, I felt rejected. I remember crying out to him for attention and begging him to show me affection. When he paid attention to the kids, and not me, that created greater

The memories of being molested were present in my bedroom.

fear. I became nervous that he may start liking my twin girls in a sexual way. I was driving myself crazy by feeding the monster in my head. The trauma of my past haunted me. When my husband and I had sex, my mind was all over the place. If he had on a certain scent, it took me back to the night of the basement. The memories of being molested were present in my bedroom. If my husband entered the bathroom too quickly, it triggered my trauma. I even started locking the bathroom door.

The little girl inside me craved attention and my husband was starving me. I started using social media as an outlet. Everyone on social media was happy (so I thought), and I was living a lie. I often threatened him with divorce to get him to change. The changes

> *It took several years before I divorced the monster of trauma.*

only lasted for a short period of time. After many let downs, I decided it was time for us to separate. During our separation, I posted sexy pictures online for attention. I needed to feel wanted. I received many comments and likes from men. It was always short lived, and I would have to go back to posting more pictures. After the comments were done, I was left alone again. I was repeating the same cycle. But it wasn't El's fault. I had not taken the steps to heal. Healing is a choice. It was my choice.

It took several years before I divorced the monster of trauma. God and therapy helped me to stop the ugly dance with it. Therapy allowed me to identify what my trauma truly was and how the loss of my father affected my relationships with men. I was finally able to mourn the loss of my father and show empathy for myself for being a survivor. I started looking in the mirror and actually seeing myself. After many years, I found my smile again. I started seeing my beauty for the first time. I no longer longed for the compliments and validation from other men, like those, "Hey, beautiful!" messages.

After ten years of marriage, God's strength gives me the ability to keep going every day. My husband didn't create the monster inside me. The monster was created the day I became fatherless. I have confidently found a way to love myself and express my needs to my husband. Little Meme still needs love and care some days. My husband knows when he needs to stop and hug me. I feel like I'm experiencing love for the first time, every time. I have a new set of tools to help me cope with life now. Healing for me meant divorcing the monster of trauma and loving myself without a blueprint. I owe it to my younger self, my kids and the woman on the other side of the door, to be a better version of myself.

Transparency and self-awareness are my superpowers. God has pulled me through the fire and turned my pain into purpose. As a marriage and family therapist, I'm able to walk with women on their journey to healing. God allows me to witness the healing journey from the other side of the window. I have founded a nonprofit called Emma's House, Inc. We work with little girls, like "Little Meme", to inspire, educate and empower them to be the best version of themselves. God is using my story to change the trajectory of women's lives forever, and I am thankful.

> *Transparency and self-awareness are my superpowers.*

For more information about Shameka and her fearless way of life, visit www.memegreenpublishing.com.

💍 SELF-REFLECTION QUESTIONS 💍

1. Describe a time when you wish you had your father. *Tip:* Do a brain dump and journal certain ages and the events connected to that age.

_____

_____

_____

_____

_____

2. How can you divorce the monster of trauma to have a healthy marriage?

_____

_____

_____

_____

_____

SELF-REFLECTION QUESTIONS

3. What are some things you can do to heal the little girl inside of you? For me, I often give myself a hug or do something I wanted to do as a kid.

_____

_____

_____

_____

_____

4. Take some time to self-reflect. What are you believing God to help you change?

_____

_____

_____

_____

_____

Chapter 5

Marital Miss

Latisha Roodbeen

"But they that wait upon the Lord shall renew their strength, they shall mount up with wings like eagles; they shall run, and not be weary; and they shall walk, and not faint."

Isaiah 40:31, King James Version

Growing up, I was the typical tomboy. I liked climbing trees, jumping fences and leaping over garages. I liked racing the boys in the neighborhood, mainly because I knew I was faster than them. I spent the other part of my time with my younger brother Kevin, playing video games. Due to my father not being around, I don't think my mom was strict on me. She was just firm because it was just her raising me. As a child, I don't remember being sad that my father wasn't around. I guess it's because I had my mom and siblings. So, I really didn't think about it until I got old enough to understand. As an adult, I realized when you're a child, the environment around you is what you view as normal. Things like me just having my mom and not my dad seemed normal to me. That's all I knew for the longest time. I had heard the term "daddy's girl", but that wasn't the case in my life.

I was "momma's girl" because that's all I had. When I had events or award ceremonies at school, it was her who I would see in the audience smiling at me. There wasn't one ceremony that she missed. I remember when I was in middle school and my school was doing the play "How the Grinch Stole Christmas." I was chosen for the part of the Grinch. I believe my mom wasn't feeling well that day. She didn't know if she was going to make it. This was the first play I was in. I was a little disappointed, but I went on with the show. When the show was over, everyone was cheering

> *I was "momma's girl" because that's all I had.*

and smiling at the wonderful job we all did that night. When I came down to greet the audience, someone took my hat off. When I turned around, it was my mom. I was so happy. I can't even explain the smile on my face when I saw her. That moment, I think I realized that's what moms do. They show up even though they may not feel the best. For their child(ren), they show up, no matter what.

My mother and father divorced when I was four years old. My father was in the Air Force, so I didn't see him much. I saw my dad again when I was six, when he brought my half-brother to my mom's house. After that, nothing. I was upset, sad and disappointed that he wasn't around. But, I buried those feelings. I never asked my mom why he wasn't there. I was young and couldn't understand. Of course, I always wondered what he was doing, where he was, or why he didn't come by. But I didn't let it bother me because of the love around me from my mom.

One day, my mom brought me an article. I was twelve years old. When I looked at it, the first thing I saw was my father's name. It stated that Thaddeus P. Draper had been incarcerated for robbing a bank. If I did want to try and find my father, I couldn't now. There was no way my mom was taking me to a scary jail. A few months into his sentence, I received letters from him. I had so many questions: *Why was he there? Why didn't he come see me? Did he want to see me?*

My godfather, Jerry, started taking me to church when I was sixteen years old. He put me in the choir and on the usher board. I loved singing more. I was baptized a year later, once I understood what that meant and how important it was to have a relationship with God. It was the teachings—not just from the pastor—but also from the elders of the church that taught me about how to conduct myself as a child. It taught me the roles of parents, husbands and wives. I learned that forgiveness can be given at any time. It's okay to forgive. Going to church, having a closer relationship with God, and being able to hear His Word helped me realize that maybe I was hurt or mad at my father for not being around. My other family members served as the shield that protected me. Because I had that shield, I didn't let it bother me that he wasn't around. My shield was my protection from any hurts or ill feelings.

> *I learned that forgiveness can be given at any time.*

After writing my father consistently, he was finally released from jail shortly before I graduated high school. I don't recall seeing him right away when he got released. He also didn't come to my graduation. I tried to drown out my pain with the loud screams coming from the audience of my older brother. I tried not to care. But, in reality, I did. I was disappointed because he was out of jail, but he didn't seem to make any effort to see me.

After graduation, I went away to college. I didn't go to church much, if at all. I pretty much only went when I came home to visit.

I was searching for that love that I thought I needed because of my missing father.

It's not like I forgot about God, but He was not at the forefront. I stayed in college for a year and a half, until coming back home to live with my mother and my younger brother Kevin. By then, my eldest brother had moved out. I was a bit promiscuous when it came to guys because I was searching for the love of a man. I was searching for that love that I thought I needed because of my missing father. I bounced from this guy to that guy, and I really didn't care. I thought if I just had sex, it would make them want to be with me, which would make me happy. Well, that was truly not the case at all. I became pregnant. The first time, I had a miscarriage. However, the second time, I wanted it to be different. I thought my boyfriend and I had something special. I told him I was pregnant, and he was disappointed. He wasn't ready for a major change in his life. I finally vented to my mother, who suggested I get an abortion. I didn't know how to feel. I was angry and sad. I felt inadequate, vulnerable and ashamed.

Looking for Love

I was trying to hold on to my dignity when I met a man at work. During our lunch break one day, I asked him why he wasn't eating.

He told me he was fasting. I inquired further because I didn't know what that meant. The more we talked and got to know each other, the more we became friends. He invited me to his church. We were quite different. I was outgoing and vocal, and he was quiet and reserved. When I went to his church, it was different from the church I attended when I was younger. I eventually became a full-time member and renewed my relationship with God. I was happy, and full of light and energy. Everything was good.

By being with him, I didn't feel like an object that a man used when he felt like it. I knew that I was important and that I deserved to be loved. After dating for a while, we were blessed with our daughter. Having a baby gave me the biggest blessing I could've ever imagined. I had a little person who needed me to care for them, love them

> *Living with him allowed me to experience a different parental perspective.*

unconditionally, and keep them safe. Soon enough, her father and I started going down different paths. I wanted to be a family and get married, and he wanted something different. By the time our daughter was six months old, we went our separate ways. We did our best to co-parent. Even though we were not together, I was, and still am, grateful that we met. Not only did I go back to church consistently, but I had my daughter.

During this time, I didn't see my father. However, I did have his phone number. We talked every once in a while. I called him and expressed how I wanted to move out, and I asked if me and my daughter could live with him. He said yes. I was shocked, but I agreed without hesitation. Living with him allowed me to experience a different parental perspective. I remember falling asleep on my dad's shoulder while watching TV, and he would fall asleep too. It was during this time that I realized how much I needed him in my life. Our relationship got stronger and I found out that I had a lot of his traits, including how I viewed things, talked and laughed. We were able to talk about the important times he missed. I wasn't mad at him. I had forgiven him. I was thankful that God put him in a position to be there for me as an adult, which was when I needed him the most. Time went on and I eventually found my own place. We still made it a point to communicate.

Life always has ups and downs, but this next turn was devastating. I was in a new relationship and had my second child. Things were looking up, that was until my mom told me news that pierced my heart. She had cancer. During this crazy time of my life, I started a new job as an administrative assistant. One particular day, one of the site managers asked me to call a few employees and invite them to a

> *Life always has ups and downs, but this next turn was devastating.*

meeting. One of the men I called had an incredibly unique last name that I couldn't pronounce. I refused to mess up his name. So, when he did answer, I only said, "Richard" and hung up the phone. Soon after, a six-foot, athletic man came to my desk, looked at me with these warm, brown eyes and said, "Okay, I'll be at the meeting." From then on, we had a running joke of him coming to my desk because I couldn't pronounce his last name.

We quickly became friends. We talked about the craziness at work, and eventually spoke about the issues we were having with our respective partners. I was still with my child's father, Ron, and Richard was married. We were both having similar issues with our partners, so it felt good that I could relate to someone. Ron and I came to terms with the fact that it was time for me to move on. He and I were definitely not on the same page. I knew I deserved more, needed more and wanted more. I just didn't know how. I did know I had to do it on my own.

I started having feelings for Richard. I was drawn to his energy, his smile, his carefree attitude, his eyes. When he looked at me, it was like he could see right through me. He saw the hurt I was trying to hide from yet another failed relationship. It was crazy because I didn't know it, didn't mean to, but I fell in love with a man who wasn't mine to have during that time. Then, out of nowhere, it happened. I believe that one kiss can tell a lot. When he placed his hands around my face, and pulled me in for the most romantic, alluring and seductive kiss, it was a wrap, as they say. I knew I wanted to feel that forever. But I also knew that I couldn't and wasn't supposed to have it. So, because I couldn't have what I wanted, I found companionship from elsewhere. I wasn't even looking for a boyfriend, but just someone else to take my mind off him. Richard wasn't happy about it. But, from where I was standing, he was forbidden fruit. So, I did my own thing. In doing my own thing, I had my third and final daughter.

A Line in the Sand

When we as women do things that we want instead of waiting on what God has for us, we make a mess of things. I wanted what I wanted, and I fought for it for a long time, three years to be exact. I knew deep down that I was 100% wrong in loving Richard. He wasn't mine to love in the first place. But my heart was overpowering my head. The love I felt was a feeling I had never felt before. As wrong as it was, I wanted him to be mine. So many times, I kept telling myself to stop the relationship. If it was meant to be, then we would meet again down the line when he was readily available. But, at the time, I was scared to be alone and scared to be without him. This man made me feel special inside and out and I didn't know what I would do without him. I prayed and asked God what I should do. I finally ended it.

It was Labor Day 2009 when I received a rather angry and nasty message from him. I went crazy. I proceeded to do damage to his vehicle. I did feel better at the time, but I was hurting. I felt used. I felt like it was a bunch of BS. I had just been a distraction for him to not deal with the problems of his relationship. However, I was so in love with this man that I knew this was the real love I was supposed to have in my life. The love that wasn't supposed to be mine had to be removed because it wasn't the right timing. I didn't understand any of that at the time, but it took a lot of praying and asking for forgiveness to make it all make sense.

It was wrong in the sense that I shouldn't have entered into the relationship knowing he was married.

Through a lot of tears and prayer, I realized the whole relationship was wrong. It was wrong in the sense that I shouldn't have entered into the relationship knowing he was married. But it taught me the biggest lesson: Wait on God, and don't listen to your flesh.

It was almost a year before we were in each other's space again. I was single. After the big blowout with his wife, so was he. I found out the angry and nasty text message that I had received from his phone was actually sent by his wife. It was a long road for us to trust each other again. If I had to go back and do it again, I would have kept it platonic, so no one would've been hurt. It was a lot of healing that had to happen for us to move on.

It was 2011 when things were much better between us. The night that he asked me to marry him, I was thinking, *Is this the right time now to do this? Can I handle being someone's wife with the free spirit that I have? Would I be able to calm that down and humble myself?* I was nervous, but I accepted the proposal. When I looked into those brown eyes, I knew no matter what, he was going to be my protector as God protects His children from all hurt or harm. This man cared for me and my little people. They may not have been biologically his, but he didn't treat them any differently. We were a blended family, but a family, nonetheless. I had what I had wanted so for so long: a loving man who loved me unconditionally, spoiled me for no reason, and treated me as a queen.

We were finally getting married. We chose to get married at the hospice facility so my mother could see our union. She was getting worse, and I was very worried. Two days after our wedding, my mother passed away. I was devastated. I felt like I lost a piece of my foundation. My rock was gone, but it was the strength that she passed on to me that kept me going. Due to my loss, my father and I grew an even stronger bond. I remember calling him and saying, "I have one parent left. I don't care if it's once a day or once a week. I need to hear your voice." From that day forward, he has done just that.

> *Two days after our wedding, my mother passed away.*

The road was not smooth. But on that road, I learned that I had to repent to God for the path that I chose because I loved a man who wasn't mine at the time. I asked for grace and forgiveness. The fatherless little girl that had her shield (mother, brothers and godfather) became daddy's adult baby girl. Now, the woman who has her own family, and made amends with her father as an adult, learned that there is truly a time and place for everything.

> *I succeeded and found out that love doesn't come from man, but from God.*

My legacies are my three daughters: Kylah, Tyrah and LaAnna. What I teach them as they grow and go out on their own is that you can do anything you put your mind to, no matter the circumstances. My journey is one of strength and perseverance. No matter what came my way, I bulldozed right over it. I grew up without my father; however, I succeeded and found out that love doesn't come from man, but from God. He shares His love by putting people strategically in your life, either for a time, reason or a season. It's up to you to decipher which is which. I am fearless because I accepted and owned my mistakes. My testimony is that I can overcome anything and that I can draw strength from the best energy source there is: God Almighty. If you are reading this, and you are going through something, know that you can overcome, as well.

For more information about Latisha and her fearless way of life, visit www.4mylegacyshop.com.

SELF-REFLECTION QUESTIONS

1. If you can relate to being fatherless, what steps of healing have you already taken and what steps do you still need to take?

___

2. How has being fatherless shaped you as a person today?

___

SELF-REFLECTION QUESTIONS

3. What was your journey to love?

4. Think about the person you are either with now or someone you are thinking about dating. Have you prayed and asked the Lord for guidance on how to go about the relationship?

Chapter 6

Worthy to Wed

Pearl Smith

"Your eyes saw my unformed body; all the days ordained for me were written in your book before one of them came to be."

Psalm 139:16, New International Version

For most of my life, being fatherless felt harmful to me. I longed to experience the love and attention from my father. My

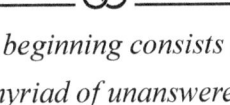
My beginning consists of a myriad of unanswered questions.

beginning consists of a myriad of unanswered questions. There is a forever void in my heart because I do not know the nature of my beginning. When I was born, my mother was sixteen and my father was seventeen. Did my parents love each other? Did they love me? I am not privy to the origin of their relationship, other than the fact it produced me. I figured since my mom was so young, my father was probably her first love. I wish I had asked more questions about their relationship when I had the chance. Sadly, both my parents are deceased.

I do remember being a little girl and not having a father. It seemed normal that most of my classmates were raised by their mothers, yet I still longed for a father. Unconsciously, I knew that even though I have never experienced a father in the home, a father was *supposed to be* in the house with the mom and the kid. No one told me that. I simply figured it out at eight years old. Besides, the books we read in school always showed a mom, a dad, children and a dog. In my mind, that was what a family was supposed to look like. This lack of validation as a young girl contributed to my insecurities. I was ugly, unattractive and worthless. I lacked value and self-respect. My mantra was if my own father did not think I was worthy, why would anyone else?

One time in third grade, while participating in a play, I had to call my classmate dad. I could not utter those words. Those words belonged to one person: *my dad*. My teachers tried to coerce me into saying my lines, which included calling this kid dad. That was too much for an eight-year-old. Shaking my head and crying, through my tears, I managed to shout, "You are not my Dad!"

Ironically, my mother never said anything negative about my father. She also did not say anything positive. She never really talked about him at all. It was as if he was a non-existent memory for her. If it were not for me, she would not think about him, *ever*. I do remember hearing that my father was on drugs, and she did not want to be a part of that lifestyle. At the time, I did not know what drugs were. But I soon understood that she and my father were never going to be a couple. I never desired them to be a couple. My biggest desire came from being a little girl who wanted a daddy.

Sometimes I wished I were white. From what my six-year-old mind could see, white fathers lived with their family. They ate together. They laughed and went on trips together. Not me. It was just me, my mother and my sisters.

> *From what my six-year-old mind could see, white fathers lived with their family.*

I now wonder what attracted my mother and father to each other. Were they high school sweethearts? Was she a one-night stand for him? Was he at the hospital during my birth? Did he deny me? How did he feel when my mom told him she was pregnant? How did she feel being pregnant? Did they break up when she decided to keep me? What kind of boyfriend was he? Why was I not good enough for him? What was my purpose, and how did I fit into this equation called life? These and many other questions plagued me. For as long as I could remember, there was always an emptiness, a missing puzzle piece. Back in those days, children didn't ask those types of questions of their parents. Rarely would parents volunteer to share their relationships with their children either. I stayed in a child's place. It was very lonely at times.

At the age of twelve, I got answers. The answers I received brought to life my true feelings of worthlessness and a whole bag of insecurity. I felt shame for a sin I had not committed. I was ashamed to be my father's daughter. I felt like an embarrassment to him. Why else would he invest in others and not in me?

I met my father and grandparents officially when I was twelve years old. Apparently, they knew I existed, but they never sought me out. My grandmother orchestrated a meeting between my father and me. I sat on my great-grandmother's couch, waiting for my father to come over. Fear nearly paralyzed me as I sat in the living room by myself. Each time the front door opened, I wondered if the person coming in was my father. Tears started to fall when I realized I truly did not know what my father looked like.

My father eventually came through the door. Imagine being introduced to your father, the one who should already *know* you. The introduction was brief. He asked my age and about my mother. Then, he left to hang out with the others who were at the house. He brushed me off. He left me in the living room by myself. That was the foundation of our relationship. He came in and out of my life periodically, leaving me emptier than I was before he showed up. We never connected on an emotional level. I never called him "Dad". It didn't feel natural.

Soon, I not only witnessed, but experienced the effects of his drug and alcohol use. He openly drank vodka and used cocaine and crack in front of me. I met his many girlfriends over the years. But not once did we ever have a conversation about *us*. He never asked me about *me*. He never went to parent-teacher conferences. He didn't know about all the times I was on the honor roll. He didn't know about all the awards I received. He never even knew about all the boys I fought out of anger. He never bothered to attend any of my graduations. He probably never even knew my birthdate.

> *He openly drank vodka and used cocaine and crack in front of me.*

Yearning for Acceptance

This estranged relationship with my father, led me down a path searching for love and acceptance in other places. I based my worth

I often poured my heart and soul into a relationship, only for them to walk away.

on how my father treated me. I was not good enough to be loved. I hated how I looked. I never wanted to look at myself in the mirror. I never felt pretty, smart, good or worthy enough for the best of anything. So, I settled. There were several men in which I tried to find my worth by being attached to them. I was loyal to them. I often poured my heart and soul into a relationship, only for them to walk away. I never wanted to have children without being married to their father, but I did. I birthed two children who experienced what I experienced: *absent fathers*. I felt guilty—and sometimes, I still do—for exposing my children to the same rejection I'd endured.

It's tough navigating this world without your father. However, it is not impossible. Yet, I questioned who would want me when my own father did not want me? I equated sex to love. I settled for relationships in which I was the primary giver. I wanted people to like me. I wanted people to think I was *good enough*. It was years before I could look in the mirror and love the face looking back at me.

> *As a single mother, I never wanted to do to my children what my parents had done to me.*

I was twenty-five when I attempted to stop looking for acceptance and validation from others. I decided to make Jesus the Lord of my life. I had been looking for my worth in others, particularly men. As a single mother, I never wanted to do to my children what my parents had done to me. Yet, I followed in those very footsteps. It was the relationship with my youngest child's father that forced me to take a closer look at my life.

We had been dating for several years, many of which were toxic. We both were unfaithful in the relationship, but my indiscretion took a toll on me. It was a turning point in my life. I was involved with a man who was married and also had a girlfriend on the side. I didn't have feelings for this man, nor was I even attracted to him. I was smitten by the words he spoke to me. He told me I was beautiful. He told me that I deserved a man who loved all of me. He made me feel wanted. Our conversation made me question the love and loyalty of my child's father. Eventually, we were intimate. I hated myself. I never thought that I would stoop that low. I was depressed. I considered suicide. I was reckless. I did not know how to overcome this. Every time I looked at myself in the mirror, I was reminded how worthless I was.

During this time, God showed me things that changed the trajectory of my life. He used my family to show His love for me.

My sister introduced me to a cousin we did not know. My sister and my cousin attended the same church. My cousin became one of my best friends and was even my maid of honor when I got married. The relationship with my cousin was essential to me being able to share my life. I shared everything with her. She, in turn, shared God with me through Bible studies and her life.

God, in return, showed His love for me. Through Him, I learned that I was wanted. I was valuable. I was worth dying for on the cross. God showed me that even though my earthly father was not present, He had been present in my life all along. *He* was my Father. I decided I would walk the rest of my life's journey embracing God being my Father.

> *I decided I would walk the rest of my life's journey embracing God being my Father.*

Even though I was now a Christian, as a human I was still broken. I still carried the sins of my parents in my heart, along with my personal sins. I don't even know if I prayed and asked God for help. All I know is that He removed the blinders off my heart and eyes. He showed me that He protected me from my father's drug and alcohol addiction. I saw my father as a broken man with his own demons. He did not know how to fight those demons. My heart softened, and I had compassion on him. He was the man God choose to be my father. So, I forgave him. I never received an apology. I simply chose to honor him as my father.

While I never called him "Dad", I did take the initiative to get to know him. I called or visited him during the holidays. I eventually visited him at his home just because. I was in my 30s when my father's heart changed toward me. He had stopped using drugs and alcohol. He was married to a Christian woman. His life was totally transformed. He welcomed my calls and visits. When I didn't call him and wish him a Happy Father's Day, he called me, sharing that none of his children had called him. Out of all his children, he *expected* me to call. My heart was broken. I promised him I would never forget to call him again.

Soon after, I met an amazing man through a mutual friend. He lived in Virginia, and I lived in Michigan. We began a long-distance friendship for a few years, then a long-distance courtship. I was not interested in having a boyfriend during the time we met. I prayed and asked God to bless me with a best friend instead.

> *I am not valuable, and I am not worth even flowers.*

Whenever possible, we visited each other. On one visit, as he was driving to our date location, he pulled over and purchased some flowers from one of the street vendors. As he handed the flowers to me, I said, "Thanks." What he said next cut to the core of my heart, and I started crying. He told me that I deserved more than a bouquet of flowers. I looked at him and saw the sincerity in his eyes. I turned toward the passenger window so he would not see the tears roll down my cheeks. *Why did he think I deserved more? Doesn't he know who I am? I am not pretty. I am not a good catch. I am not valuable, and I am not worth even flowers. Why would he say those things to me?* Even though I disagreed with him, I could tell he genuinely believed that I deserved more. I just could not fathom, nor could I accept, why he believed this about me.

After several months, I felt secure about introducing my father to my boyfriend. When they met, they instantly clicked and loved and respected each other. It was amazing to watch them build a relationship. My boyfriend later asked my father for my hand in marriage. He took him tuxedo shopping as a nice bonding gesture. Soon enough, my boyfriend started calling my father just because he wanted to talk to him. Later the next year, my father walked me down the aisle. I was honored to have him there. I felt he was proud of me as his daughter.

The Journey to Restoration

During our fourth year of marriage, my father became sick and passed away. His sickness brought back the memories of everything I had missed growing up. It was uncomfortable being in the position of his power of attorney. He had been in the hospital on life support when the doctor called me for a meeting. I was told that a machine was keeping him alive and that I needed to decide about whether to keep him on life support. I did not know about his health or his wishes. *How did I become in charge of the life of a man I barely knew?* Once again, I felt my father put me in an unfair situation.

However, God gave me all the strength I needed to make the decision, track down my siblings, and plan a funeral for the man He chose to be my father. A man I barely knew. A man I chose to honor.

> *Once again, I felt my father put me in an unfair situation.*

My husband was there with me every step of the way. This is what is amazing about my God. While I was single, I prayed for a man who would love and serve everyone, not just the people he cared about or the girl he was attracted to. I had grown up watching males only take care of women they were attracted to and it was sad to me. Every woman should feel special or worthy of being served, regardless of whether or not a man thinks she is pretty enough to take care of. I had spent so much of my time feeling left out and uncared for that this was an important characteristic for me.

Throughout our relationship, there was always this fear that I would mess up the relationship and he would leave. The first couple of years of our marriage, I lived on eggshells. I knew once he found out who I was, he would not want to be with me. He would leave. I was convinced I would be the reason for our divorce if we were to break up.

The first couple of years of our marriage, I lived on eggshells.

My insecurity led me to be overbearing. I expected to be my husband's *only* friend. I was jealous of the relationships he had with other people, men and women. Whenever he went out with his friends, I tried to make him feel bad and stay at home with me. I hated that there were other people in his life. I was scared that the people would influence him to leave me. I was also afraid that he would find someone who was better than me and leave me for that person. I was convinced that I was boring to him. Other people were more fun than me.

It's a wonder that he never left me. I remember him telling me that he was here for the long haul. I could not fathom anyone being with me for the long haul. While I waited for him to leave, my husband was constant. Maya Angelou once said, "When people show you who they are, believe them the first time." I did not believe him when he said I deserved more. I didn't believe that he loved me. I didn't believe I was the best for him. Furthermore, I didn't believe that he wasn't going anywhere. While I was waiting, God softened and changed my heart.

I prayed to God, asking Him to let me see my husband the way He saw him. Soon, I saw my husband as God's son. He was my husband, not my father. He chose me because, to him, I was valuable. In his eyes, I was worth the long haul. I was worth the commitment. I was worth the vows. I stopped complaining and started observing him. I watched his interaction with his friends, with our children, with his parents and with my parents. I saw how he loved my family, even those I have yet to love. I saw that he was everything I prayed for. God had blessed me with a man who loved everyone, not just the person he was attracted to.

> *I saw that he was everything I prayed for.*

I let my guard down and allowed him to be himself. He had already allowed me to be myself. The more I let my guard down, the more we connected. We're now able to talk and laugh and have fun together. Now when he goes out, I am okay. I look at the times that we are not together as a time for me to connect with God or with my friends. Healthy couples need space.

We've been married for seventeen years now. I still love him as much today as I did the day that we became one. Thinking back on our wedding day, the day when my father allowed me to put my arm around his and willingly walked me to my forever love, I never felt surer about anything as I felt that day. My earthly father, the one who chose drugs over me, gave me away to a man who could love me and treat me the way I deserved to be treated. For that, I am grateful.

None of this would be possible without the gentleness of my Heavenly Father. Jeremiah 29:11-13 says, *"For I know the plans I have for you," declares the Lord, "plans to prosper you and not to harm you, plans to give you hope and a future. Then you will call on me and come and pray to me, and I will listen to you. You will seek me and find me when you seek me with all your heart."* I love this Scripture. It has been useful to quote when I want to encourage others about the plans God has for their lives. This Scripture has taken on a new meaning to me. What if everything I experienced was a part of God's plan? The good, the bad and the ugly? What if God planned for me to grow up fatherless? How did this plan fit to prosper me and not to harm me?

He knew the plans He had for me even before I was born. He knew that I would long for a father. At the right time, He would supply me with one. He knew that my greatest need was my worth He showed me through His love. I was worth dying for and I was worth waiting for. My Father showed me that I did not have to lower my standards or compromise for someone to desire to be with me. This was evident in my relationship with my husband. Our first kiss and act of intimacy was on our wedding day. If I had a chance to live my life all over again, I would walk the same journey. I would choose the same man to be my earthly father.

Fatherless women, you are near and dear to me. I understand the struggles and the insecurity that comes with this pain. Whenever I am talking to a fatherless woman, I remind her that she is not her father's mistake. Like us, our fathers are human. Most of them are broken. Many of them are little boys trapped in a body designed for a man. They do not always know the importance of their presence in their daughters' lives. We do have a Father who loves us unconditionally. He sees the best in us. To Him, we are worthy. He will never leave us. We cannot rely on our biological fathers, our boyfriends or even our husbands to make us whole. That responsibility belongs to our Heavenly Father. I took a chance by allowing God into my life. It was the best thing I have ever done.

For more information about Pearl and her fearless way of life, visit www.pearlivsmith.com.

SELF-REFLECTION QUESTIONS

1. I struggled with thinking I was worthless because of my father's lack of presence in my life. What are some of your struggles as a fatherless daughter?

   _____

   _____

   _____

   _____

2. Parents are not superheroes. They are human. Consider the challenges and struggles your parents may have endured growing up. What are they?

   _____

   _____

   _____

   _____

SELF-REFLECTION QUESTIONS

3. Jeremiah 29:11 shares that God has a plan for you. Even in suffering, there is a plan. How does being fatherless work into the plan God has for you?

_____

_____

_____

_____

_____

4. How did being fatherless affect your relationship with your husband?

_____

_____

_____

_____

_____

www.ingramcontent.com/pod-product-compliance
Lightning Source LLC
Chambersburg PA
CBHW050436010526
44118CB00013B/1548